HOW TO BE A NUISANCE

A COLLECTION OF POETRY

CORI FISHER

HOW TO BE A NUISANCE

A COLLECTION OF POEMS

BY CORI FISHER

THIMBLEWEED
PUBLISHING CO.

Copyright © 2026 by Thimbleweed Publishing Co.

All rights reserved.

No part of this publication may be reproduced, distributed, or transmitted in any form or by any means, including photocopying, recording, or other electronic or mechanical methods, without the prior written permission of the publisher or author, except in the case of brief quotations in critical reviews and certain other noncommercial uses permitted by copyright law.

For Kayla

Table of Contents

Presenting the Facts	1
How to Love Me, Regardless	2
Butchered	3
Emma	4
Fishing	5
Deciding to Thrive Over a Music Video	12
West Union Avenue	13
The Business of Grievers	14
Notes App, In Order	15
The Lightning Bug	17
I've Never Forgiven God for Letting Things End	20
So Much of Survival	21
The List	22
It Counts	23
Focus—Or Don't	27
Cher, 2 a.m.	28
Rainstorm	30
Seed Snow	32
Become New	33
On Fancy Bras at 13	34
One of You	37

Dancer	40
How to Be a Nuisance	42
A Picture of my Mother and Me, Aged 26 and 6	44
Advice to My Never-Future Daughter	46
When My Mother Decides to Die	47
Translucence	52
Golden Ragwort	54
Damn This Dog	56
The Dinner Guest	57
Praise Be to Bug Bites	58
Moments of Hush	59
What It Is	60
Theoretically Better	61
U.S. Headlines – 3/27/24	63
Mary Oliver Allows It	66
In Response to "Mill Doors" by Carl Sandburg	68
The Precipice	69
What It Was Supposed to Be	70
Farewell, I'm Bound to Leave You – An Homage to Fred Chappell	71
Acknowledgements	*75*
About the Author	*77*

Presenting the Facts

They say, "You
would argue with God."
Well, of course, I would.
Who wouldn't?

I approach prayer as
a negotiation.
If I present the facts
straight,
surely,
God will see
the obvious truth—
get some sense
about them and
act right.

Although, it does seem
to be taking
quite some time.

How to Love Me, Regardless

Watch the same sitcoms
on repeat.
Don't yell much—
or stomp.

Hold your jaw softly.
Sneeze quietly.
Expect no creamer
for mornings.

Know I am up
or down.
Each time, it
is forever.

Enjoy your solitude, but
stay close.
Expect less effort
in return.

Don't be too mean
or kind.
Both are bad
for my nerves.

Butchered

I gave a five
to the baker
six fingers to the tax man
my heart to my lover
an ear to my mother
my spine to my father (again),

my belly to
the dishes
ten toes to
the dogs
and their wishes,

my teeth to the grocer
some skin to the banker
a leg
and an arm
to my job.

Now, my brain spends
the night, pushing
and grunting, birthing—
until new parts appear,
so I can pay
these debts
again.

Emma

I asked the sister of my soul
if she'd ever eaten her fill, ever satisfied
herself to the point where she
couldn't name a single thing to want.

She said, "Never—not once.
I always want something more—
more perfect."

Fishing

One day, with weather
I can't remember in a season
that has escaped me,
my stepfather took me
to a trout pond.

"It'll be easy," he said.
"They have nowhere
to run."

He was right. I hauled
fish after fish
through the stocked water,
droplets falling down
my scrawny arms.
The fish went into a
bucket, and I didn't think
of them again once the lid
closed. It was on to
the next catch, the
next praise.

Then, I hauled a good one,
slick in the sunlight—or was
it cloudy? I can't
remember.

I poked around its mouth,
searching for the hook
but came up empty—only

the line trailed from
between its hungry lips.

I gripped the line, gave it
a good tug, and felt the fish
shudder in my hand. I placed
it between my knees—for
strong grip—and yanked.

That day, I learned I could
hear a tear in another's
body.

The hook flew out
of the fish's mouth. It
clutched
a hunk of brilliant, red
organ. Blood poured
over my hand, coating
my prize
in red.

I screamed
for help.

Memory should serve me
here. What happened next?
Did the fish die in my
hand? Did my stepfather
let me see its last flops?
Or did he slip it, mercifully,
into the water, telling me

it would be just fine?
But nothing comes.

I remember only that he saw
my tears mixing with
pond muck, placed his
hands on my shoulder
as I sobbed—guilty of
ignorance, of not knowing
the art of fishing, of
murder before God and
everything else—then
that he got on my level,
looked me in the eyes,
and said, "You have a very
big heart."

That day, I learned
I had a very big heart—
and that fishing meant more
for the fish than it did for me.

The summer I turned
eighteen, I'd grown enough
to pretend that trout's
blood hadn't bothered me
much—that I never
thought about it.

I worked in an office for
room and board, though
it was only a room—

no board. My boss brought
her two children in every
day, their eyes dull against the
matte beige of easy-slide
carpet. Their color waned
as the weeks passed, so
one day, I said, "There's
a pond across the field.
Would you like to go
fishing?"

Something like life
colored the boy's
eyes. The girl watched,
waiting, learning what to
think, then straightened her
posture. "We don't have
poles," she said.

But I was eighteen
and clever and proud
to be clever, though I
haven't been clever since.
I found some sewing
thread, a ruler, and a
paperclip, used the
blunt paring knife in the
office kitchen to sharpen
the paperclip's end to
a point, making my best
approximation of tackle.

We raided
the fridge and found feta
cheese—the perfect bait.

As we three—What were
their names?—
walked to the pond,
I said, "It'll be easy.
They have nowhere
to run."

After explaining the nuances
of my ingenious contraption,
I returned to the office,
envious of their afternoon
in the sun, sure that I had
gained some award, reached
some untapped excellence.

An hour later, I stretched, then
went to check on their
progress. Two sets of eyes
met me, both ablaze with
guilt
and terror
and shame.

My pole had worked.
A fish—bluegill or perch
or crappie, the memory is
fuzzy—flopped on the grass
at the pond's edge, the
paperclip lodged in its lip,

body heaving, scales
near-dried in the heat
of the day.

The boy's eyes fell on
its small body.
"I don't know
how to do the next
part," he said, and it was
clear that he hated
the admittance.

So, I smiled, said,
"Oh, it's no big deal.
I'll handle it," plucked
the hook free, and slipped
the fish back into the algae-
covered water. I don't remember
if it swam away, but I do
know I said, "See?
It's just fine."

I wonder if those kids
learned something. I wonder
if they remember it
better or worse
than I do—or
at all.

Now, I sit at the lake's
edge with the wrong tackle,
the wrong line, the wrong
pole, determined not to learn

the proper way to lure fish.
It's peaceful, being a
bad fisherman, with barely
one bite each year.

I've learned the
best way
to fish.

Deciding to Thrive Over a Music Video

Steal a snippet,
a bite of ramen,
a bar of "Tiny Dancer."
Joy. Space.

Gulp
it
down.

Savor that
uncomfortable
expansion
of life in
your chest.

West Union Avenue

She waits upstairs
in
a white house,
old—
a corner lot
that
no one visited
today.

The Business of Grievers

I'm sorry
that I cry
when the gnat
gets stuck
in the fly trap.

I just can't stand
watching it
try to pull itself
free.

Notes App, In Order

EVOO
Yellow Onion
Carrots
Celery
28 oz Can Diced Toms
1 Can Cannellini Beans
Kale
Creamer
Dog Bones

There is nothing good to say.

624280091

Manatee

10/30 2:45pm Haircut

Section about mother on her own.

Coffee
Lotion
Meds
Water
Eggs?
Celery Seed

Half-glorious—lithe in its
lack of intent.

Bread
Walnuts

The Lightning Bug

On the railroad tracks, where
we weren't allowed to be,
he snatched a lightning bug
with his little boy hands,
took one grubby thumb
and smashed it
into his palm.

"Look!" he declared.
"See how it glows?"

A fluorescent paste of God-
knows-what—organs and
cells, most likely—shone
against his skin like paint on an
artist's palette. Then, his
index finger the handle,
his fingernail the brush,
he drew a smiling face
on the railroad track.

I cried little-girl tears,
told him
he was bad
and cruel
and mean.
After that,
after his face sealed up,

how could
he not be?

It was his name now, the proof
glowing remnants on his hands.
I knew little of mercy, so
he suffered a pain only children
inflict
upon other children.

Now, I wonder about mercy,
about grace.
How much to measure
and weigh and level with
the back of a spoon.

Is it long or short?
Does grace end once
the bad vote is cast, or
only once that vote
is defended?
Or does it end sooner,
when the first salacious
news article is consumed?
Or after that, at an
undetermined and limitless
time, after all the faults
that can possibly exist
have been uncovered
and loved
but counted?

Which of us qualify?
The boy who killed
or I who named?

Who makes that call?
Where can I reach them?

I've Never Forgiven God for Letting Things End

There comes a day
when a dog has zoomies
for the last time,
and no one marks it.

Not even
the dog.

But then, the local
stray cat saunters
up the driveway.
It stretches out,
purring,
and burrows itself
into the gravel,
sensing the danger
has passed.

So Much of Survival

So much of survival
comes down to
a rocking chair
on a tile floor,
the yellowed light
from a single bulb,

a cup of tea,

and playing tug
of war
with a pup
in that space
between
sleep
and wake.

The List

I collect ailments
as others collect coins,
stamps,
thimbles from places
long ago traveled.
For they are knickknacks,
pieces of identity
truly mine.

Panic disorder.
Morton's neuroma.
Bipolar disorder—
type 2, according to
my psychiatrist,
"All the bipolar with
none of the fun."
Two leaky heart valves,
Tricuspid and Mitral.
Palpitations.
One bad knee, yet
unnamed.

I roll their names across
my tongue, cup them in
my hands, and hold them,
keeping the list whole
and holy,
ensuring I am
who I thought I was
the day before.

It Counts

It took three days to shower,
two to brush my teeth (with
toothpaste, at least). I had run the
wetted bristles across them,
my arms too tired
to reach for the tube.

It counts.

In the shower, I
expected the water to swirl
down the drain,
stained.
But it didn't.
No one would
have seen it and thought,
It's hard to talk right now.
It takes too much breath.

It counts.

I did some of the dishes today.
Gave my dog most of his
antibiotics and took
half my own. Made dinner,
chewed through
exhausted jaws.

It counts.

When the laundry sat high
on the bed, I rumpled it
back into the basket and used
all my strength to
set it aside.

It counts.

This week, I have slept everywhere
but my own bed. The couch,
the office chair,
the daybed upstairs. I have
fretted,
fitful dreams, but still…

It counts.

For twenty-two days, an email has sat
in my inbox. I have opened it
at least ten times with the intention
of answering. But each time,
I read the words
from my therapist:
"Haven't heard from you.
Are you okay?"
And with the best of intentions,
I decide to answer it later.
Again.

This is the see-saw, the consequence
of singing to the tomato plant

on my front porch
at 3 AM
last Tuesday.
It's the opposite of can-do,
the 'little low' my medication
prevents from blooming into crisis.

But let me tell you.
It counts.

And today, as I sat on the porch,
the last baby robin
from the nest
wedged beneath my roof
toed its way to the edge of home
and jumped.

It flew, face-first, into a log
and cracked a smile
onto my face.

I watched it, so terrible
at being what it is, perch and
fall, perch and fall,
until time drew me inside
to go to work—
because no matter what
miracles of the universe occur,
the mortgage will still be due
in two weeks' time.

And when I returned to check
on him again, he had gone.
Off into the woods, into a tree
nearby, yet unseen.
I was half-happy to have not
been there
to say goodbye.

Focus—Or Don't

Stop spiraling
for one hour.
Turn on the true
crime documentary.
Breathe—
just enough.

Don't make a fuss
when the sliver of
yourself uncoils
a tiny bit.

Pretend you don't notice.
You'll scare her.

Breathe again,
but careful.
Don't get cocky.

Watch the TV murder
unfold. Feel the
cautious regrowth of
your bitten nails
begin, if only for
this gracious hour.

Cher, 2 a.m.

This is the 'showing up' part,
the late-night dance party
held via video with a
friend from the other side
of the world.

It is the 'lord, give me strength,'
the forcing of a body
to move.

Who cares that the video
crackles?
Does it matter if
only the bass seeps through
factory-set speakers?

It doesn't.

What matters is that I sing
bounce
hop
smile
through the
'I don't feel like it,'
'Just not in the mood,'
'Maybe later.'

It is that we are two
people here,
for this brief second
together, sure that
we are each alive.

Rainstorm

When it storms for two days
and your body thirsts
for rain, the ancient
bond between your cells and the
cosmos, the salt of the sweat
on your 15th July on Earth
lip knows no difference
from the salt
of the seas.

When you watch the plump
drops splash, chaotic
among the checker-mowed
grass, the freshly re-sealed
driveway, the square, trimmed
boxwoods and feel the tightness
of your clothes—not sudden,
but suddenly unbearable—you
forget that

it is midday;
this is a respectable neighborhood;
anyone could see you

because, for once, you are
alone and alive and
sovereign, the caller of
the shots, the Earth's

favorite child. One more
moment in this shell will,
surely, kill you.

So, you strip off your
clothes, traverse the front porch,
splash over the sidewalk until
your toes squidge into the
muddy grass.

You stand there, a rooted,
stark-naked tree, unashamed
and quenched for two minutes,
then go back inside and
never tell
a single soul.

Seed Snow

How strange
to be alive,
to witness
little white tufts of
seed snow
on a spring day.

Become New

Pick up the stringy-haired
little girl, the one whose
eyes will grow into yours after
days and years and periods
and breaks and renewals.

Press her chest against yours.
Hold her. Love her. Remember
her name, the one she chose
for herself in the arbor—surrounded
by laden grape vines—
and whispered
to no one.

Kiss her eyelids.
Set her down.
Let her rest, and
finally,
finally,
become
new.

On Fancy Bras at 13

In eighth grade, after
gym class, girls spilled into
the locker room. Off came
Soffe shorts, maroon and
gray tank tops. Voices chipped
against cinder block walls—some
lilting, some deepening,
all rough and foreign
to the bodies that
made them.

But four of us—
Daniella Taylor,
Marley Burton,
Arianna Moore,
and I—

slunk out of sight,
wedged ourselves into the
corners of an out-of-service
shower. Six sprayers, four
right angles, and our awkward,
unfamiliar bodies.

We undressed and re-clothed
in a flash, our noses
each stuffed in a separate corner,
the unspoken agreement that none
of us would look or speak
a binding thread.

I don't remember how
we came to be there. Surely,
there was no whispered truce.
We were not friends,
nor enemies. I imagine one
of us took the first leap, and
the others followed.

In the shower room, we became
a loosely-bound coven, creatures
of solitude in a pack.

We knew which girl
was on her period
by the way she ducked into a
bathroom stall rather than
finding her usual corner.

We knew which corner was
ours without claiming them.

Our stiff bras and cotton
Hanes briefs set us apart from
the hollering on the other
side of the wall. When we
stepped out of the shower
and left the room, no one
noticed. Our separation
didn't need acknowledgement.
It simply was.

But now, I wonder
what would have happened

had we realized the hallowed
ground we created, had we
accepted that we didn't
have to face the girls outside
to face each other.

One of You

I stepped into the glare
of the movie theatre bathroom—
popcorn kernels stuck in my gums
and a bladder filled with two hours of
prolonged excitement

Four of you stood at the sink, passing
mean-girl-glances at my speeding,
late-twenties,
beginning-to-sag,
becoming-well-loved
body
as I slammed the stall door shut.

One, two, three, four—
each separate, yet so much the same.
Two of you shared lip gloss,
smacking pink giggles at your reflections.
A scrunchie held each wrist, swapped
from this friend or that's house—
who could possibly
keep track?

Your whispers slid through the air,
wedged between the tile cracks,
and burst in a glorious cacophony.
A tune I'd heard before,
that had once escaped my lips.

When I cracked the door and raised my
eyes to meet yours—eight staring in unison
into the glow of the incandescent mirror,

your silent pact almost pushed me back. But
at the last moment,
you flowed apart at the sink
so I could wash my hands
to leave.
The only gift I could give.

I saw you see me
and look through.

The exuberance of your nails and hearts,
the sincerity of your self-absorption—for
how could there be a world
outside yourselves? You were the
epicenter of emotions. The boy
you kissed in secret behind that
broad oak tree in the schoolyard
was your greatest pain, and no
one could ever grasp your unique confusion,
your bafflement at the purpose
of the hairs on your big toe
or your nighttime sobs as you
wondered if your life meant
anything at all.

You parted it all to let me through,
the adult interrupting your vital
conversations, stealing precious seconds
of independence.

You didn't see one corner of my mouth
upturn
or the softening of my forehead
as I met my own reflection in the mirror—
an entirely different one than you
ever expect to see.

But I was once you.
I remember your secrets
and dire circumstances.

I knew that nothing would ever
matter more than this moment
because each moment of your lives
is the only one
that will ever be.

Your disregard pushed me
into womanhood,
a place I cannot navigate
but where I must reside
all the same.

My ghostliness in your presence
proved that I am
no longer one of you
and never will be
again.

But I remember you,
and I love you still.

Dancer

My mother is not a dancer.
She danced all the same.

Spinning through our living room,
bare feet brushing
second-hand rugs,
the cassette fighting its
urge to tangle as Melissa Etheridge
vowed she was the only one.

I had never seen my mother
free. She always stood
tall through a weighted back,
shackled to the service of
womanhood. Tearing one piece of
herself after another, offering
each one to my hungry
mouth, sparing a taste for
the next
demanding soul.

But as she danced,
I saw the human in her
eyes, felt the rhythm of her
blood pulsing in the drum
of her steady feet
beating the floor.
I was too young to know that

her dance was a protest,
a defiance against this life
brought before her.

A brief interlude of freedom
in an otherwise written story.

Now I understand why,
when my father walked in the door,
she was quick to turn off the stereo.

How to Be a Nuisance

Mama taught me
when your best friend calls,
says, "It's over. He finally
broke it," about a man
you've hated since
day one, you
hop in the car
without makeup,
sans purse,
with whatever gas
you have,
and go to her.

Not only do you help
her pack, but you load each
thing. Grandma's china, a half-
open box of tampons,
her good sweaters. You
make room.

Then, you settle her into
the passenger's seat, put a
Kleenex to her cheek, whisper,
"I forgot something."

You walk into the great,
gaping silence of
that bastard's house, snatch
the toilet paper from the

roll, find the reserve
in the laundry room.
Take it all.

You unscrew every lightbulb—
even from the oven
and the fridge—
wipe out the extras
beneath the kitchen sink.

You throw it all in
a box, take it out, and
shove it into the crevice
of your backseat floorboard.

When your best friend eyes
you, puzzled, and asks why,
you reply,

"To be a nuisance."

A Picture of my Mother and Me, Aged 26 and 6

You are confidantes. You are ghosts. You are the products of sweet tea and minimum wage. You are determined. You are whispered rhymes at bedtime and the scent of Vick's Vapor Rub. You are made up of mountain. You are ancient.

You have no smiles for the man behind the camera.

You are the only comforts. You are adult and child, child and adult—you do not know who is which. You are tense. You are white, or olive. You are the full spectrum of light. You are four eyes, a single set of lips, a nose. You are near-complete replicas. You are worlds apart.

You will spend a decade this way.

You are partly each other. You are mostly the other. You cling to the parts of yourself you can see. You are a misplaced fingernail, a scrap of hair, finding its way onto the wrong body. You are interchangeable.

You are translucent.

You are the summation of small triumphs. You are black sheep. You are young. You are walkers. You are readers. You inhabit the same place at separate times. You are the lack of image. You are another Saturday evening dance party, alone in the living room in your tube socks.

You are the definition of will—will do—will live—will work—will fight—will learn to love.

Sheer will.

You are one, made two, come round to one again.

Advice to My Never-Future Daughter

Don't
let your lover
turn you into their escort.

If they can see
the sadness
in your eyes
but cannot identify
your pain,

they do not see you.

They only love
the themselves
in you.

But,
if they bring you
water
when you are trying
to thirst to death,

you will not die
in their hands.

When My Mother Decides to Die

"I won't get that old," she says.
"I won't suffer to death, or lose
my mind, or become a burden."

*You deserve to be
a burden,* I think
but just look at her,
nodding.

"When the time comes,
I'll walk into the woods
or the water
and go."

Streetlamps halo
her in gold
as we walk
and talk
and muse.

"Drowning isn't so bad.
Peaceful, once the panic
stops. Did I tell you about
the time I almost drowned?"

"You did," I say, then wait
because I never quite
remember the details.

I want to hear it
again, to learn it
because so many stories
keep getting lost
when people do.

She tells me.
Something about a lake,
about her own mother,
about not being watched.
And, damn it, I can't
remember it again.
I can only feel it,
as a daughter feels her
mother's past.

The problem with being
my mother's daughter—
with being born from a
woman of her integrity—
is that she

really

means it.

I don't think she will
get old. She'll walk into
that water the second time
her memory faults.
She won't wait
for a third.

Will she call me?

Will I be invited?

Is it a daughter's duty,
her honor,
to escort her mother
out of this life?

Is it a mother's right,
her last
reclaiming of self,
to go alone?

Will my brother
join us, or are
boys both spared
and cheated
of this passage?

Will it be dawn
or midday
or the womb
of night?

Will I hold her wallet and
car keys, sit on the bank,
and watch her slip beneath
the murky water?

Knees, belly,
chest, shoulders,

chin,
lips,
eyes,
then the crown
of her head, leaving
only a ripple
behind.

Will I hold back while the
bubbles slow? Between now
and then
and the decades that
separate them—
if we're lucky—
will I grow enough
to wait?
To be so respectful?

Or will I shuffle
my feet, throw
down the keys
before bursting
into a run, thrashing
and sobbing into
the water,
begging her to
stay just a
little while
longer?

Will I take that peaceful,
dreamed-of exit

from her? Will I be so selfish?

Mom—call me.

Translucence

It is all so real; around me,
the creek runs cool and
soft, blunting stones over and over,
the same path routed by millennia.
Many men have tried to
reroute her, but she rolls on.

The robin's nest on my
porch is renewed each year—by the
same mama, I cannot tell.
Her pink-bodied babies screech,
hungry again, until the hawk
takes them all in one fell swoop.

The women who made me have
lived—are a nurse, a writer, a
policewoman, a factory worker,
a woman who forges her path
forever. They have wept and
belly-laughed. They turn the
world with weary hands, keeping
us all alive, thankless.

I observe them, absorb them,
stand in the shadows, adoration
moving my pen. They are the essence
of existence, just out of reach.

My life has been spent trying
to be as real, but it is beyond me.
So, I pen it all, grateful
to witness what breathes
in this mad place.

Golden Ragwort

March, and he stands on the porch, a hand
on his head. He gazes over fourteen acres,
all his responsibility.

Buds hug branch tips, a promise of green,
fresh life, of new beginnings reflected in the
mirror of my eyes.

Grass shoots spring forth, here and there.
He knows what's coming. Eight-hour days,
three days a week.

It takes work to keep nature in check.

"Damn this grass."

April, and he stands on the porch, a hand
on his head. He gazes over fourteen acres,
all his responsibility.

The weeds have grown ankle-high, then
knee-high. Golden Ragwort encircles our
home, a crown of suns. All for me.

He sweats out a clear path around the house
but will not cut the yellow crowns, ignores
them with
a cursing sigh.

He doesn't need to be asked.

"I left you some flowers."

May, and he stands on the porch, a hand on his head. He gazes over fourteen acres, all his responsibility.

The suns are sullen, half-empty of lost petals. He walks to them with a scythe, then turns away. It is not time.

He leaves me all beauty, knowing it will be more work later. Ticks, snakes, hours and days, scorching sun each await.

He waits 'til every petal drops.

"Anything for you."

Damn This Dog

Wait until Mom changes
into her coziest t-shirt,
until Dad swerves out
the driveway for his
night shift.

First, ensure the porch
light is burned out.
Bonus points if the
bathtub drain is broken.
Bonus again if the
hose head is loose.
Extra bonus if
the moon is new,
the world encased
in a dark sock.

Find a skunk.
Piss it off.
Come home.

The Dinner Guest

Love someone who notices
your bowl, sparse and
meatless, floating with
only a few potatoes, two
carrots, due to the
unexpected dinner guest.

Watch as his eyes
shift, as he ladles
roast from his own
bowl to yours. Listen
to his firm whisper:

"Don't you ever starve
yourself so someone else
can eat."

Learn to hear him.
Dear God, if it takes
twenty years,
believe it—

But only half, for
his belly is now
emptier for you.

Praise Be to Bug Bites

Praise be to bug bites,
the proof-of-life itch
separating me from
sterility.

Welts along my arms, my
legs, one above my brow,
swollen with refusal.
They will not be ignored.

Keep those plaster walls;
I no longer want them.
Give me heat.
Give me biting wind
seeping through cracks
in the winter.
Let the wasp dance along
my spine as I sleep
in a humid haze.

The scent of must, the cedar
intermixed with dog hair.
This is life.
It will not placate,
nor bend,

nor hold.

Moments of Hush

All I can think of is
heavy snowfall. The first
time in late autumn
when you realize
all the bugs have died or
gone to sleep.

The hope that floorboards
don't creak when sneaking out
for a nighttime smoke
at seventeen.

The moment the dog takes
his last breath behind the vet's office,
right before the doctor whispers,
"He's gone now."

The crying out for reason.
The deep, inner reaching
for answers
about why you are
the way you are
and how you might manage
to become something else.

What It Is

As I walk by
the lake, my love
of ten years by my
side, full from lunch,
blood hot from
a day in the sun,
with green-algae
water dried to my
skin, I think, *Savor
this. Feel it all
so you can write
a poem.*

Then, I grin.
How silly of me
to forget that
poems emulate
this.

That is why they
are written
in the first place.

Theoretically Better

The Buddhists say, "Look
into the eyes of your
worst enemy—

the cruelest politician,

those who throw rocks
at cats,

the nurse who
tenderly
breaks the bones of
newborns
in secret—

and
learn to
love them."

That is the path to
enlightenment.

I swear, I have tried—
more than once, or twice,
or a baker's dozen times.
But when I hold their
faces in my mind's
eye, consider the flutter
of a pulse in their temples,
the wisps of hair their

mothers tucked over
and over
behind scrubbed ears
and try to open my heart,
my compassion turns
to ash.

I turn
to ash—
become rage, ancient and
full-bodied, become
inhuman, forgetting
the meaning of
empathy.

In these moments,
we have the most
in common—these
monsters and I—and
I can't imagine
anyone
has ever been
enlightened.

U.S. Headlines – 3/27/24

"The reason I think most things don't change is that if stupidity were oil, we'd be the richest country on the planet."
— Lewis Black, *Me of Little Faith*

SunChips Releasing
Limited-Edition Flavor
For 5 Minutes
During Solar Eclipse.

$1.13 Billion Winning Mega
Millions Lottery Ticket
Sold In New Jersey.

The Internet Is Losing
It Over Donald Trump Selling
An American-Themed Bible
For $60.

'Titanic' Door That Saved
Kate Winslet
Sells For $718,750,
Beating Indy's Whip.

New HIV Cases
Linked To Shuttered New
Mexico Salon That Offered
'Vampire Facials.'

Why Birds Are Not Using Your Birdhouse.

Education Department Botches
College Financial Aid.
Again.

Pub Of The Year Loses
Award Due To Nazi
Memorabilia Display.

Over One-Third Of
US Adults Would Move
To Foreign Country If Able.

Retired Grandmother Still Owes
$108,000 In Student Debt
40 Years
After Taking Out Loan.

Deceased Man's Body Found
In New York Water Supply
After 25 Days, Authorities
Declare Water Safe
For Consumption.

SWAT Team Raids
Innocent Family Over
Stolen AirPods
Dropped On Their Street.

New York City Police Officer Fatally Shot
During Traffic Stop.
Texas Ranches Ravaged By Wildfires Face

Long Recovery.
Baltimore Bridge Collapses, Six Presumed Dead.
Trump Is Turning the January 6 Coup Leaders Into Fascist Martyrs.

5 Things To
Be Grateful For
Even When The World
Is Falling Apart.

Mary Oliver Allows It

Forgive yourself—
you are not Robin Hood.

Run up this credit
card, then the next.
Fix teeth, have the old dog's
bulging eye removed, count
the cans of tuna in
your cupboard—

you scoundrel, with
your two bags of beans

—etch portraits of
Mandela, of Lenin, of
Mangione into potatoes
before they meet the
boiling water (leave
no trace of idolatry,
should they come
knocking).

While the mash bubbles
for supper, search for
bankruptcy lawyers
near you.

Will they come pull
the tooth?
How many landfills to

search for the dog's
putrefying eye?
What a waste of time,
of money,
to demand your two
bags of beans—
to send boots and
thick-walled tires.

You and I are not
Robin Hood. But rather
than burning it all to
keep it from their vile,
gluttonous hands, we
will be the ones who ensure
they come to claim
empty cupboards—
our neighbors belly-round,
laughing, with
tears in their eyes.

In Response to "Mill Doors" by Carl Sandburg

We stand at the mill
doors, knocking,
knocking,
the number of shuffling
feet stamping the ground
growing.
The raps of our knuckles
curl into the
pounding
of fists.

Soon, one of us
will have lost enough,
will have tipped the scales,
and we will barge in
to free you.

The Precipice

1/19/25

It is the night
before
inauguration day, and
I feel there is much
to do
to write
to save
to free
to prepare—
things I have today
that I won't
tomorrow.
So, I must cherish
them now
in these waning hours
before the fight
begins
and ends.

What It Was Supposed to Be

The night after
we started making plans
to leave,
I dreamed I pulled up
the hulking chestnut tree
from the soil of my
great uncle's house—
where it has always been,
where I have always
loved it—and
broke it from its roots,
knowing it was finally time
to bring it home.

Farewell, I'm Bound to Leave You – An Homage to Fred Chappell

You, who are older than
Saturn's rings,
precursor to bones,
mother of coal,

I was one of you,
forever.

I was born of your stripped back,
have bent with honor as you
erode—lost a quarter inch
each year as you do.

But once, a man
invented money. The next
day, a million more wanted
it. Even you could not
stop them. Now,
I must go.

Who will call the
lightning bugs?
Who will measure the new
buck's antlers—first a thimble,
now a blade?

I have broken my promise.
I cannot suffer to keep it;
this, I have learned
with the shamed, open
eyes of adulthood.

Now, I turn
toward Costa Verde—
How green are you?
Do your trees shiver through
bitter winters? Do false
springs tease the flowers
dotting your hills?

Do you have hills?

How do I say 'vegetarian'
in Portuguese? What about:

"My dog has food allergies."

"I've been on this medication for decades."

"How much for these tomatoes?"

"It's pronounced Apple-at-cha."

"Please welcome me."

Will honeysuckle speckle
your roads in June?
Where can I pick crabapples
in autumn?

Do muscadines grow
in Madeira?

No, I didn't vote for him.
Yes, this is home now.
I'm fine, thank you.

My husband read that we
will be greeted by the
murky green of Atlantic
waters. He'd hoped for blue.

But I praise the mother
of women, of mountains, of
misplaced souls for letting
my hand touch water that
laps against the shores of home.

I wonder what boulders
will have shifted in us
if I return.

Acknowledgements

It took a tremendous amount of support to bring this collection into the world. I'm sure many people have unknowingly influenced these poems, but specifically:

Thank you to my husband, Lyndin, for this life and your love.

Thank you to Emma Hanes for your delirious belief in me over the past 15 years.

Thank you to Dora Porcaro and Sandra Isaacs for being my beta readers and support system on the other side of the world. And thank you to Natalie Seabolt for being my beta reader and support system in the library stacks.

Thank you to Gemma Wilson and Hayley Shipton for working so hard on the cover and layout.

And finally, thank you to my mother, Annessia, for continuing to teach me how to be a nuisance.

About the Author

Born and raised in Southwest Virginia, Cori decided as a young teen that she wanted to become a writer who lived in a cabin in the woods. After graduating from Hollins University, falling in love with working in kitchens, and a stint in the veterinary field, she recalled that childhood dream. Cori now lives and writes in a cabin in the woods, alongside her husband and three dogs. How lucky is she?

Cori also dabbles in historical fiction and writes horror under a pen name. Cori has been a professional manuscript editor for 12 years.

www.corifisher.com

www.ingramcontent.com/pod-product-compliance
Lightning Source LLC
LaVergne TN
LVHW010427070526
838199LV00066B/5950